# A POCKET GUIDE TO THE DOCTRINE OF THE TRINITY

Joshua Ensley

A Pocket Guide to the Doctrine of the Trinity

Copyright © 2021 Joshua Ensley. All rights reserved.

Pronomian Publishing LLC
Rock Hill, SC 29715

ISBN: 979-8-9851529-0-6

Publisher grants permission to reference short quotations (fewer than 300 words) in reviews, magazines, newspapers, websites, or other publications. Request for permission to reproduce more than 300 words can be made at www.pronomianpublishing.com/contact.

Unless otherwise noted, Scripture quotations are from The ESV® Bible (The Holy Bible, English Standard Version®), copyright © 2001 by Crossway, a publishing ministry of Good News Publishers. Used by permission. All rights reserved.

Cover Design: Daniel Solomon Kaplan

# A POCKET GUIDE TO THE DOCTRINE OF THE TRINITY

Joshua Ensley

# CONTENTS

Why This Book? ................................................................ 1
Why the Doctrine of the Trinity is Important ................... 5
A Brief Explanation of the Doctrine of the Trinity ............ 7
God the Father ................................................................ 17
God the Son .................................................................... 21
God the Spirit ................................................................. 35
Closing Thoughts ............................................................ 51

## INTRODUCTION
# WHY THIS BOOK?

In 2010, I was first introduced to what I now call pronomian theology.[1] While I've seen how this view of Scripture has brought about many positive reforms within Christianity, I have also recognized some concerning issues beginning to arise within this movement. In an attempt to reform the Church back to what we pronomians believe to be the law-positive faith of the Apostles, a few babies were thrown out with the bathwater. Sadly, often included in this band of babies was the doctrine of the Trinity. Now, this is not to say that all former and current pronomians are non-trinitarians; it is to say, rather, that it was a common trend in the early days of this reformation to second-guess the doctrine of the

---

[1] Pronomian theology is a theological position held by Christians who affirm the ongoing validity and applicability of the Torah (i.e., The Law of Moses), in addition to the authority of the entire Old and New Testaments. The term pronomia is the antithesis of the term anomia (ἀνομία): lawlessness, iniquity, disobedience, sin. The term ἀνομία is a combination of two Greek words: α (against) & νόμος (that which is assigned, usage, law). Linguistically, pronomia reflects "pro-law" in contrast to "anti-law" of ἀνομία. Common, notable beliefs & practices among pronomians include: Seventh-Day Sabbath observance, observance of biblical festivals of Passover, Unleavened Bread, Pentecost, Day of Trumpets, Day of Atonement, and Feast of Tabernacles, observance of the biblical (Leviticus 11) dietary laws, & physical circumcision of males on the 8th Day. For further information about pronomian theology, see https://joshuaensley.org/2021/01/06/what-is-pronomian-theology/.

Trinity and even throw it out as unbiblical. Today, I stand as an unapologetic trinitarian from the perspective of both Sola Scriptura (Scripture Alone) and Tota Scriptura (All Scripture), and I have taken it upon myself to give a defense of this critical and foundational doctrine in hopes that you are strengthened in your faith with regards to the nature of the God whom you claim to serve.

This book will follow a simple format wherein I will begin with my defense as to why I believe the doctrine of the Trinity is important, followed by a systematic approach to explaining the primary claims and confessions of trinitarianism. From there, we will examine from the witness of Scripture how all three of the persons of God (Father, Son, & Spirit) are equally eternal, powerful, and worthy of worship as God. I will then share my closing thoughts as we conclude this book.

## What This Book Is and Is Not

Though this book will serve as a defense of the Trinity doctrine, its ultimate purpose is to be an abbreviated guide for you to maintain an understanding of the doctrine as you grow in your faith. My hope is that this book can sit on your shelf or in your office and serve as a guide when you are questioned about the nature of God or when questions arise from within yourself.

This book is not intended for those on the scholarly level, but for the layman as a bridge between scholarship and applicability for our lives. For scholarly work on the topic, I highly recommend Dr. James White's *The Forgotten Trinity* and St. Augustine's *On the Trinity*. It would be senseless of me to attempt to replicate such marvelous works on this topic when these options are still in print and available almost everywhere. Rather, I want to offer the Church something simple to accompany each believer on their everyday life journey: an abbreviated guide to this essential doctrine.

From here, we move into the journey of exploring the doctrine of the Trinity and addressing the questions that so many have about the inner workings of God's nature. I hope this book will help you see not only the beauty of what God has done for us in the redemptive work of Christ and the indwelling of the Holy Spirit but also the truth of who God is.

# CHAPTER 1
# WHY THE DOCTRINE OF THE TRINITY IS IMPORTANT

The doctrine of the Trinity is important first and foremost because God has chosen to reveal the doctrine to us through his Word, thereby making it a biblical doctrine. The Bible forces us into the doctrine of the Trinity because the text speaks clearly on the concepts and understandings of God's triune nature as preserved by scholars within Christendom for thousands of years. I do, however, recognize that the statement I just made will surely cause some of you to shudder. Still, I cannot deny this claim in regards to the Trinity any less than I could deny this claim in regards to the biblical doctrine of monotheism, for both are expressed within the text of the Bible. I pledge to do my best to defend this claim in the coming parts of this book, but first we must first recognize its importance if we are to recognize its concepts.

Without submitting to this doctrine, the Christian is in danger of compromising on critical, theological truths. For example, the Jehovah's Witnesses deny the Trinity through an appeal to Christ's created nature, which paves the way to heretical doctrines claiming that Jesus was merely the created Archangel Michael. This idea completely undermines dozens of New Testament Passages that state clearly that Jesus is an uncreated being. The Church of Latter-Day Saints denies the Trinity by appealing to the position of polytheism (belief in many gods) and thereby opens the door to a need for extrabiblical works (the Book of Mormon) in order to guide the life of the Mormon. Even many within the Messianic/Pronomian movement deny the Trinity by appealing to subordinationism (that Jesus is not equal with God) and thus are forced to accept that Christ is not Lord of all but just Lord of some.

## Why the Doctrine of the Trinity is Important

Because I believe that God's revelation within the Bible forces the Trinity doctrine upon us, I must acknowledge that doctrines that exist in contrast to the Trinity doctrine are heresies, as the Church throughout history has so deemed them. However, I do not believe that all those who believe in such doctrines are heretics because I distinguish the outright rejection of this doctrine from theological ignorance. I believe that every Christian is a theologian by nature and that we are to make continual efforts to sharpen our theology. I hope that this book serves as but one tool to bring about this sharpening in your faith journey.

Though one of today's hot phrases is "Don't give me theology; give me Jesus!", a lack of proper theology is the very opposite of what God intended for us through his word. When the Apostle Paul opens his letter to the Philippians, he explains that his prayer is not that the Philippians are filled first with money, housing, or food, but rather with knowledge and *all* discernment.

> And it is my prayer that your love may abound more and more, with knowledge and all discernment, so that you may approve what is excellent, and so be pure and blameless for the day of Christ, filled with the fruit of righteousness that comes through Jesus Christ, to the glory and praise of God.
> —Philippians 1:9-11 ESV

Christians, without a proper understanding of such a foundational doctrine, I believe that we are significantly hindering our witness of Jesus to the godless and dying world. Only through a critical, accurate, and biblical knowledge of him, both in regards to our relationship with him as well as who he is, can we best share him with others.

# CHAPTER 2
# A BRIEF EXPLANATION OF THE DOCTRINE OF THE TRINITY

When discussing, teaching, or explaining a topic so critical to our faith, it is important that we first define terms that will be used frequently throughout the discourse. I believe that the doctrine of the Trinity has many terms that are often misunderstood, misrepresented, or are confusing among Christians. This misunderstanding or confusion within the Church has a lot to do with why many non-Christians fail to have a proper understanding of this doctrine as well, for many atheists look to Christians in their research of the Church's beliefs. For the sake of this writing and my attempt to represent this doctrine faithfully, I will offer here a brief glossary of terms that will be used throughout the remainder of this book in an effort to represent the doctrine consistently and accurately.

- **God**—the central deity of the Bible as revealed to Moses in the Tanakh by the proper name יהוה (YHWH; Yahweh); referred to commonly within the Tanakh by multiple Hebrew terms, notably אֱלֹהִים (elohim; God) and אֲדֹנָי (adonai; My Lord(s)). Referred to commonly with the Septuagint (Greek translation of the Tanakh; abbreviated as LXX) as κύριος (kurios; Lord; used in place of the divine name יהוה and in general usages) and θεός (theos; God).

A Brief Explanation of the Doctrine of the Trinity

- **Being**—the substance of God; it is that which makes him "God." God's being is eternal, omnipresent, omniscient, unique. Contrary to human beings and our human nature, God's being is not limited by time, space, or knowledge; God's being is that he is infinite (unlimited) while his creation (us, the universe) is, by nature, finite (limited).

- **Person**—that which makes someone (in this case, God) *who* he is. When used alongside the term *being* in reference to God, the term *person* dictates the revelation of God's personal character rather than his divine nature and essence. Taken from the understanding of the Latin *persona* and the Greek *hypostasis*.

I will be following the model from Dr. James White's division of the doctrine of the Trinity into three foundations, as expressed in his *The Forgotten Trinity*, as I continue to explain this doctrine using the aforementioned terms. Please refer to this brief glossary if you become confused as to what I am trying to communicate.

## Foundation One: Monotheism

Monotheism is what separated ancient Israel from their surrounding neighbors in the Ancient Near East. Most surrounding tribes and nations in the ANE operated either as polytheists (many gods), pantheists (everything is god), henotheists (adherence to a particular god from among multiple), or a mixture of the three. Monotheism asserts that there exists one single god and that no other deities exist above, beside, or below that god.

## A Brief Explanation of the Doctrine of the Trinity

Trinitarians believe in the existence of one single deity—namely יהוה (YHWH; Yahweh) as expressed in the text of the Bible.[1] The authors of both the Tanakh[2] and the New Testament, as well as Jesus himself, affirm that biblical faith is necessary monotheism, and trinitarians do not deviate from this. Though many opponents of the doctrine of the Trinity make the claim that trinitarians are polytheists (more accurately, *tritheists*[3]), that is not the case when considering how the terms above are defined. Trinitarians believe that God is one *being* and that his *being* is shared by three divine, equal, eternal *persons*; I will explain this further in foundation two.

As I stated in chapter one, I believe that God has chosen to reveal this doctrine to us through his word, thus making this a biblical doctrine. How I believe he has revealed this foundation of the doctrine through the Bible can be found in classical passages of the text, from both the Tanakh and the New Testament. The Shema (Deut 6:4-9) is the classical call to monotheism found within the Bible and is the foundational assertion of who God is and who he expects his people to be.

---

1   Some scholars and historians suggest that ancient Israel practiced henotheism between their period of polytheism and landing in monotheism, but that topic is better covered by Moshe Weinfeld's *Deuteronomy 1-11* (Anchor Bible, 5).

2   The TaNaKh is an acronym made from the first letters of the Masoretic Text's traditional three sections of the Hebrew Bible (Torah—the Law; Nevi'im—Prophets; Ketuvim—Writings), known sometimes as the Old Testament. I prefer to use the term *Tanakh* over the *Old Testament* due to the latter sometimes communicating the false idea that this section of the Bible is no longer applicable or to be seen as a distinct set of scriptures with no theological connection to the New Testament.

3   Tritheism is a form of polytheism which affirms the existence of three distinct gods.

A Brief Explanation of the Doctrine of the Trinity

> "Hear, O Israel: The Lord our God, the Lord is one. You shall love the Lord your God with all your heart and with all your soul and with all your might."
> —Deuteronomy 6:4-5 ESV

Jesus quoted verse 5 of the Shema in Matthew 22:37 when asked which of the commandments in the Law was the greatest; he followed up by quoting Leviticus 19:18, claiming it was the second greatest commandment (to love your neighbor as yourself). Jesus's callback to the Shema confirms that the gutter between the two testaments did nothing to change the principle of necessary monotheism as expressed in the Tanakh. Besides Jesus, we have numerous New Testament authors echoing the call to monotheism (see 1 Timothy 2:5, Romans 3:30, 1 Corinthians 8:6, James 2:19).

Again, I must stress the necessity of monotheism in the doctrine of the Trinity. When one denies this pillar, we find them in similar places as the Mormons, for they believe that there are many gods and that Yahweh and Jesus were merely two of the total number of existing deities, and that is not an accurate reflection of this doctrine. Rather, trinitarians confirm the existence of Yahweh alone existing as one *being* in three separate *persons*, which brings us to foundation two.

## Foundation Two: There Are Three Divine Persons

I have found that this foundation is the central location of the most misrepresented, misunderstood, and miscommunicated part of the Trinity doctrine. As I explained in foundation one, trinitarians confirm monotheism, but we then have a contradiction between foundation one and foundation two unless we define the term *person* as I have in chapter two.[4] By defining *person* as that which makes someone *who* he is rather than *what* he is, we can reconcile the idea of a single God existing in three respective *persons*.

Now I would like to address a common misunderstanding of the personhood of God. It seems that most laypeople within the Church today who claim to be trinitarians actually are modalists if pressed. Modalism is a Christian heresy[5] that, on the surface, seems to be what trinitarians mean by trinitarianism; but rather, modalism is a form of monarchianism, which claims that God operates in the "modes" or "manifestations" of the Father, the Son, and the Holy Spirit at particular times. Modalism says that God can switch between these modes of expression but remains one single *person*. On this view, God throughout the Tanakh was acting as the Father while leading Israel through the wilderness, God throughout the incarnation as Jesus was acting as redeemer, and God throughout the post-resurrection New Testament as the Holy Spirit was acting as the comforter or advocate. The problem with this view is that there then exists one *being* and *person* expressing itself in various ways, and that is not what the Bible teaches concerning the nature of God. People who use the analogy of $H_2O$ being able to exist in three different states of matter (solid, liquid, gas) are actually promoting modalism rather than trinitarianism because $H_2O$ remains one distinct chemical substance (being) regardless of how many times it transitions into different modes.

---

4   Remember, refer to my glossary in chapter two regularly to ensure that you are understanding terms as I have defined them.
5   Modalism was condemned by Tertullian (c. 213 *Tertullian Against Praxeas* 1, in Ante Nicene Fathers, vol. 3) and Dionysius (c. 262 CE) and was generally regarded as heresy by mainstream Christianity after the 4th century. For more on this, see Britannica, T. Editors of Encyclopaedia. "Monarchianism." *Encyclopedia Britannica*, July 10, 2015.

Instead of God operating in different modes, Trinitarianism says that God is one *being*, just as I am one being, but that his being is unique in nature, existing in three divine, equal, eternal *persons* who are completely distinct from each other. I will not attempt to offer an analogy for his personhood because analogies appeal to the created, and since God's personhood is a completely unique personhood, no appeal to the created can sufficiently represent it. However, we can see throughout the text of the New Testament that each person of the triune God is represented as having the same being while sometimes having different duties in the redemption process.

Some will still remain opposed to the idea of the equality of the persons by arguing from a select few verses in the New Testament, most notably John 14:28. The redemption process required that the Son relinquish his equality with God the Father, not in regards to *being*, but in regards to glorification, so that he could be made a human servant and die for the sins of his people, which is why Christ can say that the Father was greater than he was during the incarnation.

> You heard me say to you, 'I am going away, and I will come to you.' If you loved me, you would have rejoiced, because I am going to the Father, for the Father is greater than I.
> —John 14:28 ESV

The Jehovah's Witnesses will be quick to say here that this is clear proof that Jesus is therefore not divine because the Father is God and Jesus is not God. However, in the context of this passage, we can see that Jesus is not speaking of his personhood, but rather concerning his place in the process. Jesus temporarily emptied himself of his glorification that he shared with God (Phillipians 2:6) prior to the creation of the world (John 17:5), and became lower than the angels (Hebrews

2:7). His appeal here is that the Son is, at that point in history, lower in regards to glorification than the Father. If we were to say that this passage is an indicator of the personhood of the Son being inferior to the Father, we would be ignoring the remaining entirety of John's gospel, as the entire point of his writing was to show how the eternal, all-powerful Logos[6] of John 1 became flesh (John 1:14) and revealed to us who God is in human form (John 14:9).

While I believe that this foundation is where most people misunderstand the Trinity doctrine, I do think that a proper understanding of the biblical text, as expressed here in this section, reconciles the seemingly contradictory claims. Once again, the Trinity doctrine affirms the existence of God—one *being*—who exists as three unique *persons*.

## Foundation Three: The Persons Are Co-Equal

This foundation has already been covered slightly in the concluding paragraphs of the previous section. Still, I would like to use this section to take a closer look at some particular verses within the New Testament, which clearly show that each person of the Trinity is co-equal (and by extension co-eternal), beginning with the prologue of John's gospel.

> In the beginning was the Word, and the Word was with God, and the Word was God. He was in the beginning with God. All things were made through him, and without him was not any thing made that was made.
> —John 1:1-3 ESV

---

[6] Logos is the English transliteration of the Greek λόγος. The word λόγος is used in John's prologue (John 1:1-14) to explain the Son prior to his incarnation as the divine reason behind all that exists in this universe.

## A Brief Explanation of the Doctrine of the Trinity

John opens verse one with a recalling of Genesis 1:1, but it relates here not to the act of creation, but to what existed prior to the creation, namely the Logos—the philosophical concept of reason in regards to God's existence. John first appeals here to the preexistence of the Logos and then explains its role in the act of creation in verse three. The contemporary reader, having already read Genesis 1, would expect to read, "In the beginning...God," but rather than God being the focus of John 1, the Logos is. We can then conclude that John is first claiming that the Logos existed prior to the creation events of Genesis 1, necessitating that the Son is divine in nature and eternally preexistent.

Further in verse 1, we see John explain that the Logos was in the presence of God, literally "with the God." John sets the foundation here with the claim that everything that Jews believe that God did in the creation of the universe was done alongside the Logos—the *person* of the Son—not apart from it. He explains further in verse 3 that all things were created through the Logos rather than apart from the Logos. This, then, necessitates that the Son is the creator God Yahweh spoken of in Genesis 1, proving that he is not only preexistent but also omnipotent (all-powerful).

We are now faced with a choice: deny monotheism and set aside foundation one, or recognize that the being that is God existed and exists eternally as separate persons. As I said in the beginning of this book, we are forced into the doctrine of the Trinity; God has revealed his completely unique nature to the world through his word: he is one being, he exists eternally as three persons, and one of those three persons—the Son, the Logos—took on human nature and dwelt among his people, fully revealing the mystery of the Messiah by the Spirit (Eph 3:1-6).

Evidence also exists within the text that the Spirit—the third person of the Trinity—is also of the same being. In what I believe is the best example of the explicit stating of the Spirit's being, we see Peter condemn Ananias for lying to the Spirit.

> But Peter said, "Ananias, why has Satan filled your heart to lie to the Holy Spirit and to keep back for yourself part of the proceeds of the land? While it remained unsold, did it not remain your own? And after it was sold, was it not at your disposal? Why is it that you have contrived this deed in your heart? You have not lied to man but to God."
> —Acts 5:3-4 ESV

Here we have Peter condemning Ananias for lying about his keeping of some of the proceeds of the church. He clearly expresses that Ananias has lied to the *person* of the Spirit but then repeats himself in verse 5 by claiming that Ananias lied not to men but to God. Notice that Peter does not say that Ananias lied to the *person* of the Father, but to the *person* of the Spirit and to God—of whom the Spirit is the third person. Many people fail to see this assertion of Trinitarianism because they misunderstand God's nature; they are ignorantly modalists. That is, they believe that the Father is the Son is the Spirit, but that is not what this chapter has demonstrated from Scripture. Rather, The Father is God, the Son is God, and the Spirit is God, so lying to any one of the persons of the Trinity means you have lied to God, but not that you have lied to one of the other persons. I could continue to give examples on the distinction between the persons of the Trinity, but I will leave that for the coming chapters of this book where I address each person and their confirmations of divine being individually.

## Conclusion

Though a work of this length could never match an explanation of the doctrine of the Trinity as well as works like White's *The Forgotten Trinity*, I do believe I have been exhausting in my attempt to address and correct some misunderstandings and misconceptions of the doctrine, and that is a sufficient goal for me as someone still working to become a scholar himself. I hope that with an understanding of the terms I defined so early on in this book, you now have a better grasp of what I mean when I say that I am a Trinitarian and better understand the gravity and necessity of holding to such a biblical doctrine.

As we continue through the coming chapters, we will examine each person of the triune God (Father, Son, & Spirit) individually from the perspective of Sola Scriptura (Scripture Alone), beginning with God the Father.

# CHAPTER 3
# GOD THE FATHER

Now that we have covered the importance of the doctrine of the Trinity and a brief understanding of the doctrine, we will now examine the divinity of each of the persons of the Trinity, beginning with God the Father. This chapter will be the shortest since practically nobody within Christian circles debates this point. The idea that the Father of the Trinity is a divine person is foundational for not only the New Testament revelation of the Trinity but also the entirety of the Bible. It seems, though, that the hang-up with many of those who object to the doctrine of the Trinity is not that God the Father is a divine person, but that trinitarians confess that he is but one of *three* divine persons of God.

## God as Father in the Tanakh

The idea of Yahweh (God) as Father exists within the Tanakh more so metaphorically than compared to its metaphysical understanding within the New Testament. Ancient Israel understood God to serve as their metaphorical Father, notably in his role as redeemer from bondage in Egypt, and this understanding is reflected in a number of texts. Here are but a few:

> Look down from heaven and see, from your holy and beautiful habitation. Where are your zeal and your might? The stirring of your inner parts and your compassion are held back from me. For you are our Father, though Abraham does not know us, and Israel does not acknowledge us; you, O LORD, are our

> Father, our Redeemer from of old is your name.
> —Isaiah 63:15-16 ESV

> When Israel was a child, I loved him, and out of Egypt I called my son.
> —Hosea 11:1 ESV

> Father of the fatherless and protector of widows is God in his holy habitation.
> —Psalms 68:5 ESV

Though Yahweh was not seen as a literal father to the nation of Israel, he was, in effect, a father figure to the nation, as the nation's existence was dependent on him establishing it, protecting it, and expanding it.

## God the Father in the New Testament

Once we find ourselves within the pages of the New Testament, we see Jesus repeatedly refer to God as the father of his people. Just within the Sermon on the Mount, Jesus refers to God as Father 17 times.[1] Though the idea of God being a father to his people was surely a part of the Jews' understanding of God, Jesus introduced a more metaphysical understanding of God as Father and that was echoed by the Apostles in their later writings. Even the opening line of Christ's model prayer reflects God's fatherly relationship to us before reflecting his divine power.

---

1  See Matthew 4:22; 5:16,45,48; 6:1,4,6,8,9,14,15,18,26,32; 7:11.

> Our Father in heaven, hallowed be your name. Your kingdom come, your will be done...
> —Matthew 6:9-10 ESV

It was the objective of the Son not to appear as a mighty warrior king—though many expected such—but as a bridge across the endless gap of humanity and its creator. By becoming the God-Man, Jesus the Son was able to facilitate a relationship opportunity with humanity and God as sons and daughters to their Father. Later, when speaking to the church in Rome, the Apostle Paul explained that living for God now grants us sonship rather than enslavement:

> For all who are led by the Spirit of God are sons of God. For you did not receive the spirit of slavery to fall back into fear, but you have received the Spirit of adoption as sons, by whom we cry, "Abba! Father!"
> —Romans 8:14-14 ESV

Referring back to Christ's prayer, God as Father in the New Testament still, though, calls on his divine nature, even if it prioritizes his fatherly nature. While praying in John 17 regarding his coming crucifixion, Jesus the Son prays to God the Father to petition that the Father glorify him (Jesus) in his presence, which he shared before creation:

> I glorified you on earth, having accomplished the work that you gave me to do. And now, Father, glorify me in your own presence with the glory that I had with you before the world existed.
> —John 17:4-5 ESV

In order for Jesus to have experienced glory in the presence of the Father before the creation, the Son must be eternal—as we saw in Foundation Three of the past chapter—the same way that the Father is eternal. The only difference we have now is that the Son has emptied himself for a little while to redeem humanity (Phil 2:7)—a concept that we will discuss in depth within the next chapter.

## Conclusion

As I said in the introduction of this chapter, this will surely be the shortest and least-debated section of the teaching because of the inherent understanding of Christians that God the Father is divine. Regardless, the argument for this thesis—that God the Father is divine—is necessary for a sufficient defense of the Trinity doctrine, as a non-divine being sending the divine Son would be quite a head-scratcher.

# CHAPTER 4
# GOD THE SON

We have arrived at my defense of the claim that Jesus of Nazareth is the second person of the Trinity, fully divine and preexistent in his being, Lord of all. Had I been writing this book ten or fifteen years ago, this would have been one of the easier parts of my defense, as most everyone (aside from groups like the Jehovah's Witnesses and Mormons) held to this belief as much as they held to the belief that God the Father is divine. However, over the past ten or fifteen years, skeptics have entered into our churches and we are now faced with significant numbers of believers (sadly) denying the divinity of Jesus. I stand firm on the belief that a denial of the Son's divinity is found rooted in the rejection of one or more of the foundational pillars of the doctrine of the Trinity. Whether it be the denial of monotheism, the denial that God exists in three persons, or the denial that the three persons are unique and equal, those who deny the divinity of the Son have surely denied one or more of those foundations. My aim here is, then, to exegete from the text of the New Testament the reality that God the Son—Jesus Christ—is divine, eternally existent, and equal with the Father and the Spirit.

## John's Appeal to Jesus as Divine in His Gospel

If you have spent any time in critical New Testament studies, you will probably have noticed that each of the four Gospel accounts have an overarching theme.[1] John's gospel begins and ends with the claim that Jesus is the incarnate Son of God, completely divine, preexistent, and Lord of all. John's prologue (1:1-18) paints the picture of the Logos of God preexisting with God (v1), being God himself (v1), creating all things (v3), and then becoming flesh to dwell on earth among his people (v14). These claims of the prologue are the lens through which John intends his audience to read the remainder of his account.

> In the beginning was the Word, and the Word was with God, and the Word was God. He was in the beginning with God. All things were made through him, and without him was not any thing made that was made.
> —John 1:1-3 ESV

There is a nuance within the Greek language of verse one that is difficult to translate into English. The word in question is εἰμί (eimi; to be) and is being used by John in verse one in the imperfect tense. The reason this is important is because John had a choice of two Greek words to use here: εἰμί or γίνομαι (ginomai; to come into being). John chose to use εἰμί in the imperfect tense in verse one, and the imperfect tense of the word εἰμί communicates the idea of existing without regard to a time when that existing began or ended, as do all imperfect tenses.

---

[1] Though the justification for this claim is exhaustive, I will gloss over the main themes in the event that you are curious and want to read further. Matthew's Gospel account aims to have the reader understand Jesus as the Son of David, the coming King of Israel. Mark's account aims for the reader to understand Jesus as the suffering servant of Isaiah's prophecy who dies for the sins of the world. Luke's account aims for the reader to understand the historical Jesus and the geographical stretch of the Gospel. For further study on the main themes of these Gospels, I would recommend the *New International Version Application Commentary* series for each book.

Here is an example of imperfect tense in English for the word "play":

Perfect: I played tennis yesterday.
Imperfect: I was playing tennis yesterday.

The perfect tense example expresses the action of playing with a beginning and an end; that is to say that it was a temporal action. The perfect tense of the verb communicates the action as having begun and ended. However, the imperfect tense gives no indication of me having begun playing or ceased playing yesterday; I could have been playing tennis the prior day and continued through yesterday and currently am playing today while making the claim, and you could not determine from that sentence alone a point of beginning or end of my action. The imperfect tense in both Greek and English grammar aims not to designate a beginning or an ending to an action, but simply to state that the action was happening.

By John employing the imperfect tense of εἰμί when saying that "In the beginning was (εἰμί) the Word," he intends for the reader to understand that the Son was already existing (εἰμί) in the beginning and that there was not a time when the Son ceased existing. Had John said, "in the beginning became (γίνομαι) the word," he would have been appealing to the creation of the Son because the perfect form of γίνομαι expresses temporality—a time when the action of being began. However, John *does* use γίνομαι in regards to the Son in verse 14 when explaining the incarnation.

And the Word became (γίνομαι) flesh and dwelt among us,"
—John 1:14a ESV

By the particular choices that John makes in regards to which verbs and their tenses to describe the Son, he shows in verse one that the Son has always existed (εἰμί) with God and as God but *came into existence* (γίνομαι) in verse 14 as the incarnate God-Man. It was the intention of John to express both the preexistent nature of the Son as well as his incarnation into our reality. He chose particular Greek verbs and tenses to express such an amazing truth about the nature of the Son—that he was always existing with God and as God (v1) and would become flesh (v14) for a time. The remainder of his gospel account must be read through this lens lest his readers misunderstand the life, ministry, death, and resurrection of the Son.

I find it necessary, also, to bring up the fact that John ends his gospel account with Thomas having understood the intended theme of the book while living through the actual events:

> Thomas answered him, "My Lord and my God!" Jesus said to him, "Have you believed because you have seen me? Blessed are those who have not seen and yet have believed."
> —John 20:28-29 ESV

John begins the narrative of his gospel account by explaining that the Son is divine, eternal, and equal with God; John ends the narrative by detailing Thomas's recognition of the truth expressed so eloquently within the text itself: that Jesus—the Son of the Trinity—is both Lord and God.

## Passages Used for Yahweh Reappropriated for the Son

There are various New Testament passages quoting the Tanakh passages addressing Yahweh. Remarkably, the New Testament authors have reappropriated such passages to refer to the Son. By reappropriating these passages for the Son, the New Testament authors are equating the person of the Son with the being of God, not the person of the Father or Spirit. We must remember that the division of Father, Son, and Spirit was something revealed to creation in the incarnation, not necessarily in the passages of the Tanakh. That is not to say, though, that we cannot find evidence of the Trinity in the Tanakh, but that the full revelation of the Trinity was concealed to our ancestors and was revealed fully by the incarnation and ministry of the Son.

In one of the greatest assertions of the Son as the divine God, the Apostle Paul reappropriates a passage from Isaiah 45 concerning Yahweh for the Son. Speaking of the incarnation of the Son, Paul says this:

> Have this mind among yourselves, which is yours in Christ Jesus, who, though he was in the form of God, did not count equality with God a thing to be grasped, but emptied himself, by taking the form of a servant, being born in the likeness of men. And being found in human form, he humbled himself by becoming obedient to the point of death, even death on a cross. Therefore God has highly exalted him and bestowed on him the name that is above every name, so that at the name of Jesus every knee should bow, in heaven and on earth and under the earth, and every tongue confess that Jesus Christ is Lord, to the glory of God the Father.
> —Philippians 2:8–11 ESV

> By myself I have sworn; from my mouth has gone out in righteousness a word that shall not return: "To me every knee shall bow, every tongue shall swear allegiance."
> —Isaiah 45:23 ESV

Before diving into the original passage of Isaiah 45, I would like to explain a critical detail in verse 6 of this passage in Philippians. The word in question is μορφῇ (*morphe*; one's form or essence) and is usually translated as *form* in many English translations, but the word μορφῇ is a difficult word for our contemporary English audience because *form* tends to be a word we use to describe outward appearances. For example, as a baseball coach, I often examined and helped improve the *form* of my players—the way they threw the ball, ran from base to base, swung a bat. But in doing so I was not appealing to their essence or nature as a human being; rather, I was appealing to that which is physical and outwardly expressed. The Greek word μορφῇ is not concerned with that which is physical and outwardly expressed; the word for that is σχῆμα (*skaema*), and Paul uses it in the very next verse to explain Christ having "been born in the *likeness* of man…" (2:7). Christ was physically and outwardly a man yet maintained his divine nature. What Paul is saying in 2:6 is not that Jesus simply appeared outwardly as God, but that Jesus possesses the unique qualities of God that makes God who he is.

Concerning the original passage of Isaiah 45:23 from which Paul was pulling, one can clearly see that the original passage is speaking of the being of God and that every person of the Earth will bow to him and swear allegiance. By reappropriating this text from Isaiah to the Son, Paul is equating the Son Jesus with God. Further proof that this reappropriation is affirming the divinity of the Son is found within the actions noted that will be done to the Son—namely, the bowing of every knee. God alone is the only being worthy of this kind of worship and allegiance, and by reappropriating this passage for the Son, Paul is affirming that the Son is worthy of this worship, thereby confirming that he is God. If we say, then, that the Son is simply acting as an agent, as many unitarians[2] have argued, we are faced with the problem that God has now gone against his own word in saying that no created being shall ever be exalted to receive glory, honor, and praise due only to himself:

> I am the LORD; that is my name; my glory I give to no other,
> nor my praise to carved idols.
> —Isaiah 42:8 ESV

The very same book now being reappropriated to the Son by the Apostle Paul is where we find God decreeing that he will never give his glory to another man or idol. It makes sense, then, that rather than the Son being a created being who was exalted to the position of glory and praise, the Son is the God to whom all glory and praise is duly given. And though he humbled himself to the place of man in his incarnation (Phil 2:7; John 1:14; Hebrews 2:9), he has been exalted back to the glory that he shared with God the Father (John 17:5). Now we can address passages in the New Testament, specifically the book of Revelation, where the Son is exalted, worshiped, and given glory just like God the Father.

> "I am the Alpha and the Omega," says the Lord God, "who is
> and who was and who is to come, the Almighty."
> —Revelation 1:8 ESV

---

2   Unitarianism is the belief that God exists as one person and one being. Unitarians believe that Christ is a created being and has been elevated to the status as shown in the New Testament, not that he possessed equality with God in preexistence.

> "Behold, I am coming soon, bringing my recompense with me, to repay each one for what he has done. I am the Alpha and the Omega, the first and the last, the beginning and the end."
> —Revelation 22:12 ESV

Here we see a passage of scripture in Revelation 1:8 where God the Father says that he is the alpha and omega, the beginning and the end, but then we see that same statement echoed by the Son concerning himself at the close of the book. Either we have to acknowledge that God has given his glory and praise to another, thus violating his own decree in Isaiah 42:8, or we must recognize that the Son is and always has been God the Son, eternally equal with God the Father.

### Jesus Claims that He Is God

Within the Gospel of John, Jesus makes seven "I AM" statements to his audiences.[3] To an audience of contemporary Christians reading the New Testament in English, this may not seem rather significant. However, the significance is found in the Greek text behind the English translations.

When Jesus makes these "I AM" statements, he is not simply saying that he is X or Y; rather, he is invoking the divine name of Yahweh by his emphatic use of the phrase ἐγώ εἰμι (I AM). In English, our pronouns and verbs are separate words, but in Greek (and many other languages), pronouns are woven into verbs as prefixes or suffixes. For example, to say "I eat" in English is to use both the pronoun "I" and the verb "eat." But in Spanish, to say "I eat," one simply says, "como." Within the word como is the suffix *o*, which designates first person

---

3   See John 6:35, 41, 48,51; 8:12; 10:7, 9, 11, 14; 11:25; 14:6; 15:1, 5.

singular. The word *comer* is the root word, which is parsed into como (*com-o*). So by saying this one word, the speaker is able to say an entire sentence. However, if the speaker wishes to be emphatic about his claim of eating, he can add the independent pronoun *yo* (I) in front of the word; the resulting translation would then be, "I I eat." Do you see how that is an unnecessary double pronoun? Though it is unnecessary and sounds strange to English-speakers, this emphatic repetition is used when the speaker intends to convey emphasis on his action.

Now let's take that understanding back to Greek. In Koine Greek (the language in which the New Testament was written), one can say "I am" by simply saying "εἰμί." The word εἰμί (the same verb used by John in John 1:1) means "I am", as the pronoun is woven into the verb as is done in Spanish. However, Jesus chose to use ἐγώ (I) εἰμί (I am), emphatically repeating the "I" pronoun. This is significant because in the Septuagint—the Greek translation of the Tanakh that was used by many of the Jewish people in the 1st century—the phrase ἐγώ εἰμί is used in Exodus 3:14:

> God said to Moses, "I AM who I am." And he said, "Say this to the people of Israel: 'I AM has sent me to you.'"
> —Exodus 3:14 ESV

The phrase ἐγώ εἰμί held extreme weight and would have been recognized by any Jew at the time as an appeal to his own divinity. By claiming to be divine in his seven "I AM" statements, the Son is authoritatively saying that he is the God who told Moses "I AM who I AM" in Exodus 3:14. Evidence of his intent can be found in the following verses where the Jewish leaders immediately seek to kill him because they recognize that Jesus is claiming to be God. Had the Son wanted to convey the simple message that he was a good shepherd, he could have employed the simple εἰμι (I am) rather than deliberately using ἐγώ εἰμι.

Though an exhaustive work on the claims of deity by the Son is beyond the aim of this book, it was important that we address it, as it is simply one more piece of evidence used to demonstrate the biblical fact that Jesus—the Son of the Trinity—is God, and made sure to claim it publicly.

## Jesus Accepts Worship

This section is similar to the section on the reappropriated passages section in that some of those passages are reappropriating worship to the Son originally given to God, but there are other passages within the New Testament where Jesus is clearly accepting of worship from his followers. The first passage was already mentioned in the section covering John's appeal to the divinity of the Son, but it is again appropriate for this section.

> Now Thomas, one of the twelve, called the Twin, was not with them when Jesus came. So the other disciples told him, "We have seen the Lord." But he said to them, "Unless I see in his hands the mark of the nails, and place my finger into the mark of the nails, and place my hand into his side, I will never believe." Eight days later, his disciples were inside again, and Thomas was with them. Although the doors were locked, Jesus came and stood among them and said, "Peace be with you." Then he said to Thomas, "Put your finger here, and see my hands; and put out your hand, and place it in my side. Do not disbelieve, but believe." Thomas answered him, "My Lord and my God!" Jesus said to him, "Have you believed because

you have seen me? Blessed are those who have not seen and yet have believed."
—John 20:24-29 ESV)

Thomas has been known traditionally as the "doubting disciple" because of his refusal to believe in the resurrection of Jesus unless he sees and feels it for himself. Once Jesus appears to Thomas and gives him empirical evidence of his resurrection, Thomas immediately recognizes the truth that his Lord and God was standing before him in glory (v28). But instead of rebuking Thomas for addressing Jesus as Lord and God, Jesus immediately recognizes Thomas's belief as a good thing. Many critics will say here that Thomas is not referring to Jesus as both Lord and God but that he is addressing the Son with "Lord" and the Father with "God," but that is reading into the text (eisegesis) rather than reading from it (exegesis), as there is nothing grammatically to suggest that Thomas changes his direction of speech from one target to another. Further evidence of this can be found when John falls before an angel (a created, non-divine being) in the book of Revelation:

> I, John, am the one who heard and saw these things. And when I heard and saw them, I fell down to worship at the feet of the angel who showed them to me, but he said to me, "You must not do that! I am a fellow servant with you and your brothers the prophets, and with those who keep the words of this book. Worship God."
> —Revelation 22:8-9 ESV

Had Jesus simply been a created being that had been resurrected by God, he would have been forced to respond to Thomas the way that the angel responded to John. The fact that Jesus accepts this worship and praises Thomas makes it clear that Jesus is not only worthy of worship as the Son, but also he accepts and encourages it.

In various other passages throughout the New Testament, we see praise and honor given to the Son in worship. Though Jesus does not explicitly accept it in the text, the giving of worship to the Son is clearly demonstrated and accepted by God:

> And I heard every creature in heaven and on earth and under the earth and in the sea, and all that is in them, saying, "To him who sits on the throne and to the Lamb be blessing and honor and glory and might forever and ever!" And the four living creatures said, "Amen!" and the elders fell down and worshiped.
> —Revelation 5:13-14 ESV

In this passage, we have every creature in Heaven and on Earth worshiping both the one who sits on the throne (God the Father) and the Lamb (God the Son). The phrase "every creature in heaven and on earth" is a way of saying every created being, for both the angels and hosts of heaven are created as well as the creatures of the Earth. Notice then that the Lamb (God the Son) is distinguished from all of the created beings both above and below while simultaneously receiving that which is due only to God. It is clear, then, that the Son is not only fully divine but also is worthy of and accepting of all praise, honor, glory, and worship as God.

## Conclusion

To echo the introduction of this chapter, I am saddened that so many people have abandoned their belief that Jesus is divine when the biblical evidence is so clear. Some find the idea of the incarnate Son being divine a problem in light of both the Tanakh and New Testament, but I believe the reality of Jesus not being divine would prove much more difficult given the claims made within the New Testament. Remember, the full revelation of God given to us came not with the penning of the New Testament, but with the incarnation, and the authors of the New Testament were simply writing their accounts years later with such a perspective already in mind. If we try to read into the text that Jesus was a created being and not worthy of honor, praise, glory, and worship, we might as well abandon the entirety of the New Testament, for it is not a body of works that allows for such a belief. And if you find yourself considering that very abandonment, I pray that you continue to seek God and his truth in this matter.

# CHAPTER 5
# GOD THE SPIRIT

The personhood of the Holy Spirit has become, I believe, the most abandoned or overlooked attribute of God within orthodox Christianity in recent decades. With the rise of the charismatic movement in the 1960s, little by little meaningful and accurate representations of the personhood of the Holy Spirit began to disappear from the pulpits of our churches in an effort to separate ourselves from the dogmatic teachings and representations concerning the Holy Spirit by the charismatic churches. But in an effort to distinguish orthodox Christianity from the chaotic charismatic movement, the church has allowed itself to minimize or even downright abandon the personhood, individuality, and ministry of the Holy Spirit. Without sound teachings on this topic from the pulpit for the past sixty or so years, and with the norm now having become that men and women of the church are no longer expected to partake in theological training in Sunday/Sabbath school or intentional theology lectures apart from the morning sermon, we find ourselves in a world where it is not uncommon for professing evangelicals to say, "Well I don't think the Holy Spirit is really a person; it's more like a force of God." This concerns me.

I have taken it upon myself here, then, to write a defense of the divinity and personhood of the Holy Spirit—that is to say that I intend to demonstrate from the Bible that the Holy Spirit is not just some active force of God, but that he is the third person of God's being, existing from all eternity past, coequal with God the Father and God the Son, and continually active in the redemption process of mankind to its creator. I will do so by appealing to three particulars from the text—the equality expressed of the Spirit with the Father, the equality expressed of the Spirit with the Son, and the operational ministry of the Holy Spirit.

## The Equality Expressed of the Spirit

It seems that most people today who deny the personhood of the Holy Spirit believe him to be merely a force of God that is less than equal to the Father and the Son. However, the text of the New Testament contains instances where the Holy Spirit is given the same attributes given to the Father and the Son, which are used in defense of their equality. I, myself, used various texts in chapter four of this book to demonstrate that the Son is equal with the Father, and the same attributes within those texts about the Son are seen throughout the New Testament in reference to the Holy Spirit.

In John 1, we read that the Son has existed eternally with and as God before the creation of the universe, making the Son equal with God the Father in reference to his eternality. No created being shares in an eternal nature with the Father and the Son, for all other beings were created in the beginning (John 1:3). However, the author of Hebrews, when speaking of the perfect sacrifice of the Son for the purification of sins, makes mention of the eternal nature of the Holy Spirit:

> For if the blood of goats and bulls, and the sprinkling of defiled persons with the ashes of a heifer, sanctify for the purification of the flesh, how much more will the blood of Christ, who through the *eternal* Spirit offered himself without blemish to God, purify our conscience from dead works to serve the living God.
> —Hebrews 9:13-14 ESV (emphasis added)

By using the term eternal (αἰωνίου) to speak of the Holy Spirit, the author of Hebrews has thus equated the Spirit with both the Father and the Son, for nothing other than God is eternal. If we are to believe that John 1 provides proof that the Son being eternal necessitates that he is equal with the Father and is God himself, we must then follow suit in believing that the Spirit here is affirmed to share in that same equality and divinity.

Consider then, also, that if the Holy Spirit were merely a force that has been sent to the Earth to accomplish particular tasks in the past and now in the present, that force would be acting in some sort of agency, much like an angel sent from God to speak on God's behalf, and would not be eternal in its own independent nature (like an angel). The existence of a force *from* God would be entirely dependent on the existence *of* God, making it a contingent being. But the Spirit is clearly eternal as shown in Hebrews 9, necessitating that the Holy Spirit is not contingent on anything. Since the Holy Spirit is independent, eternal, and commits to sentient personal acts and behaviors (as we will see in this chapter), it seems as though the Holy Spirit is a personal individual with a will much like some sort of super angel, and all of that seems contradictory to the idea that the Holy Spirit is merely a force from God, as that idea seems more akin to God acting as some sort of ventriloquist. But in all of these cases, a force sent from God would not actually be God, for no agent sent by a sender is in equal nature to its sender. King David (and the rest of the kings throughout Israel's history) was seen as God's representative while sitting on the throne in Israel, and even personally claimed that he was an agent sent in the name of God during his encounter with Goliath:

> Then David said to the Philistine, "You come to me with a sword and with a spear and with a javelin, but I come to you

> in the name of the LORD of hosts, the God of the armies of Israel, whom you have defied."
> —1 Samuel 17:45 ESV

Even though David came in the name of the LORD—that is to say that David was representing God in agency—he was not seen as God himself, nor was his being equal with God in any sense. Likewise, the angels who were on Earth in God's stead were not equal with God in any sense. John, as he was being told all that would unfold in his revelation, even tried to bow at the angel's feet and worship, which the angel condemned:

> I, John, am the one who heard and saw these things. And when I heard and saw them, I fell down to worship at the feet of the angel who showed them to me, but he said to me, "You must not do that! I am a fellow servant with you and your brothers the prophets, and with those who keep the words of this book. Worship God."
> —Revelation 22:8-9 ESV

It is clear, then, that if the Holy Spirit is merely a power sent from God or an agent acting in his stead, it would not share in the equality of being any more than David or the angels. Rather, it seems clear that the New Testament demonstrates that the Holy Spirit is equal in his being with God, eternal, and thus is God just as much as the Son is God.

Equality of the Spirit with God the Father and God the Son can also be seen in the baptism of Jesus. During the baptism, we see the Father, the Son, and the Holy Spirit all involved simultaneously and with no indication that the Spirit is anything less than equal with the other two.

> And when Jesus was baptized, immediately he went up from the water, and behold, the heavens were opened to him, and he saw the Spirit of God descending like a dove and coming to rest on him; and behold, a voice from heaven said, "This is my beloved Son, with whom I am well pleased."
> —Matthew 3:16-17 ESV

In this passage, we see the person of the Son being baptized, the person of the Father blessing the baptism of the Son, and the person of the Spirit actively coming to rest upon the Son. The symbol of a dove expressed characteristics of gentleness and peace rather than judgment. The descent of the Spirit like a dove confirmed the coronation of Jesus as Israel's Messiah, for he would now carry out the work of his ministry in the power and presence of the Spirit. He is now the one who is to baptize with the Spirit (Matt 3:11), who will be led by and empowered by the Spirit (4:1), who will usher in the Messianic age through the Spirit (12:18-21), and is now anointed by the Spirit for his public ministry. Through all of this, the Holy Spirit is seen within the ministry of Jesus as an active person with personal qualities, not some robotic force or angelic agent.

Aside from the baptism of Jesus, there exists another passage within Matthew that seems to be a significant claim to the equality of the three persons of God. In what is known as the Great Commission (Matt 28:18b-20), Jesus commands his disciples to spread the message of the Gospel to all nations, baptizing them in the name of the Father, Son, and Spirit:

> Go therefore and make disciples of all nations, baptizing them in the name of the Father and of the Son and of the Holy Spirit, teaching them to observe all that I have commanded you. And behold, I am with you always, to the end of the age.
> —Matthew 28:19-20 ESV

It is important to note that Jesus does not command the disciples to baptize in the *names* (Grk. ὀνόματα; plural) of the Father, the Son, and the Holy Spirit, but in the *name* (Grk. ὄνομα; singular). In what seems to be the most pro-trinitarian statement from the Son, Jesus in one statement invokes the distinctiveness of the three *persons* of God's triune nature while simultaneously recognizing their complete and utter equality of *being*.

However, I would commit a disservice to scholarship without disclosing that a great many scholars theorize that this passage in its original form reads "make disciples *in my name*." Put forth first by scholar F. C. Conybeare[1] (1856-1924), the argument is supported by the quoting of the passage multiple times by Eusebius of Caesarea (265-339) as having read "make disciples *in my name*." This is considered to be evidence of Eusebius having quoted from an earlier manuscript not in existence today, as there is no evidence in the MSS that the reading would not be in the trifold name. Our earliest extant manuscripts (Sinaiticus & Vaticanus), written in the 4th century, both include the trifold name. However, the absence of any manuscript containing "in my name" can be explained by the fact that the emperor Diocletian in his persecution of the Christian church ordered all sacred books to be burned in 303 CE. It is quite possible that the only surviving manuscripts are those that have been altered into the traditional trifold

---

1  F. C. Conybeare, "The Eusebian Form of the Text of Mt. 28:19."

reading. However, it is also entirely possible that Eusebius was quoting from an altered version of a single manuscript available to him or that he was paraphrasing the original trifold name and that the overwhelming uniformity across the wide distances and languages (aside from one late Hebrew manuscript dated to 1385 CE[2]) of our tradition is the original reading of the passage. Because of all this, though I hold to a trinitarian view as I believe to be expressed throughout the rest of the New Testament, my entire stock cannot be put into this passage alone, nor can it serve as a certifiable proof text of my position.

In an earlier passage of John, Jesus directly refers to the Holy Spirit not as an unequal agent or force from God, but as a paraklete. This is significant when one considers the contextual meaning and usage of the term:

> And I will ask the Father, and he will give you another advocate (Grk. παράκλητος), to be with you forever, even the Spirit of truth, whom the world cannot receive, because it neither sees him nor knows him. You know him, for he dwells with you and will be in you.
> —John 14:16-17

Jesus uses the unusual Greek term παράκλητος (*parakletos*) to describe the Holy Spirit. The "helper" or "counselor" comes from this Greek word unique to John (John 14:16, 26; 15:26; 16:7; 1 John 2:1) and is difficult to translate, as no one English word has the exact same range of meaning. Older English versions translate it as "comforter," but that seems to suggest a sympathetic mourner. "Counselor" is too broad, as it could suggest contexts like "marriage counselor." "Helper"

---

2   This is known as Shem Tob's Hebrew Manuscript of Matthew.

or "assistant" is inadequate as it suggests a subordinate rank. "Advocate" is preferred as it conveys the meaning of a legal representative, as a legal context is certainly present in John 16:5-11. But it is of most importance that Jesus says that the Father will send *another* advocate (παράκλητος), for 1 John 2:1 later says that Jesus was the first advocate (παράκλητος) sent to us by the Father:

> My little children, I am writing these things to you so that you may not sin. But if anyone does sin, we have an advocate (παράκλητος) with the Father, Jesus Christ the righteous.
> —1 John 2:1 ESV

The Son was the first advocate sent by God and is now sending a second advocate. This means that the ongoing ministry work of the Holy Spirit within the lives of the believers is not only a continuation of the ministry work of Jesus himself but also that the Son and the Spirit serve equally alongside one another in earthly ministry. God the Son was sent by God the Father as the first advocate for the people of God, and when God the Son completed the work of his earthly ministry, God the Father sent God the Spirit to continue the work of his earthly ministry, not in his stead, but as an independent person who actively regenerates (Jn 3:5), teaches (Jn 14:26; 1 Cor 2:13), distributes spiritual gifts (1 Cor 12:11), forbids (Acts 16:6-7), and intercedes (Rom 8:26-27).

How, then, can we read the words of the New Testament that confirm that God the Son is a personal being independent of God the Father while still God in *being*, yet in the same breath claim that the Holy Spirit, who actively does those same things and more, is not a personal, independent, equal person of the Trinity? We would be hard-pressed to make this argument, I believe, in light of the equality expressed within these texts. Perhaps it is the temptation to read the Tanakh in isolation, not through the lens of the revelation of the incarnation, that has caused many to see the Holy Spirit as a force or agent. I have spoken with personal friends who have claimed that they cannot believe in the personhood of the Holy Spirit because that truth is not directly revealed through the Tanakh in isolation of the Christian perspective. I agree that the doctrine of the Trinity, or at least the doctrine of the personhood of the Holy Spirit, may be difficult to understand with an isolated reading of the Tanakh. However, if we were to apply that same principle to the Tanakh in regards to the doctrine of justification, of substitution, of incarnation, we would also be forced to abandon such fundamental and necessary beliefs.

I would argue that Jesus and the New Testament authors make it clear that Christians do not have such liberty of reading the Tanakh in isolation apart from our revelation of Christ and his incarnation. The incarnation is the hinge of history—the moment when that which had been hidden from those of other generations was made known to us (Eph 3:1-13)—and through that lens we are able to know and understand the complexity of God's nature as made known to us in both testaments, even within the texts of the Tanakh which did not aim in their initial pennings to reveal what we now know. That makes for a nice transition into my final defense.

## The Operational Ministry of the Holy Spirit (OT vs NT)

Even non-trinitarians will recognize that the "Spirit of the Lord" operated in many ways throughout the Tanakh. I believe, however, that a New Testament, New Covenant perspective lens through which we now read the Tanakh will unveil even more truth concerning the Holy Spirit's ministry within the Tanakh than what the original authors may have even known while penning the words.

There exists a paradigm throughout the Tanakh where the Holy Spirit would come upon appointed individuals for a specific task and would enable them to do that task, but this resting of the Spirit on the person or persons was not a permanent state of being in comparison to the permanence of his indwelling in our present time. I would like to inspect a few passages from different eras of the Tanakh to better demonstrate this pattern:

> The LORD said to Moses, "See, I have called by name Bezalel the son of Uri, son of Hur, of the tribe of Judah, and I have filled him with the Spirit of God, with ability and intelligence, with knowledge and all craftsmanship, to devise artistic designs, to work in gold, silver, and bronze, in cutting stones for setting, and in carving wood, to work in every craft."
> —Exodus 31:1-5 ESV

We see here Bezalel was filled with the Holy Spirit by God so that he could be empowered with ability, intelligence, knowledge, and craftsmanship. Bezalel would later be employed by Moses for the equipping and decoration of the Tabernacle (see Ex. 35:30-35).

Later within the Torah, Moses was in need of help judging Israel and settling disputes. God instructed Moses to gather seventy men of the elders of Israel and bring them into the Tabernacle so that he could fill them with the Spirit to assist in bearing the burdens of the people:

> Then the LORD said to Moses, "Gather for me seventy men of the elders of Israel, whom you know to be the elders of the people and officers over them, and bring them to the tent of meeting, and let them take their stand there with you. And I will come down and talk with you there. And I will take some

of the Spirit that is on you and put it on them, and they shall bear the burden of the people with you, so that you may not bear it yourself alone."
—Numbers 11:16-17 ESV

During the time of the Judges, God would fill specific individuals with his Spirit in order for them to rule over Israel and to defeat their enemies:

> But when the people of Israel cried out to the LORD, the LORD raised up a deliverer for the people of Israel, who saved them, Othniel the son of Kenaz, Caleb's younger brother. The Spirit of the LORD was upon him, and he judged Israel. He went out to war, and the LORD gave Cushan-rishathaim king of Mesopotamia into his hand. And his hand prevailed over Cushan-rishathaim.
> —Judges 3:9-10 ESV

Even King David was aware that the presence of the Holy Spirit within his life was a temporary indwelling that could be taken from him by God:

> Cast me not away from your presence, and take not your Holy Spirit from me.
> —Psalm 51:11

The most notable temporary presence of the Holy Spirit is, I believe, his dwelling on top of the Ark of the Covenant within the Holy of Holies. Upon the construction and dedication of the Temple under King Solomon, the "glory of the Lord" came down, consumed the burnt offerings, and filled the Temple (2 Chronicles 7:1-3). But years later, prior to God bringing in the Babylonian army to defeat and enslave Israel because of their idolatry, the Holy Spirit left the Temple, effectively abandoning Israel to their enemies:

> Now the glory of the God of Israel had gone up from the cherub on which it rested to the threshold of the house.
> —Ezekiel 9:3 ESV

> And the glory of the LORD went up from the midst of the city and stood on the mountain that is on the east side of the city.
> —Ezekiel 11:23 ESV

The theme of the Tanakh was that the Holy Spirit dwelt temporarily both within specific people to accomplish specific tasks and within the Temple itself. Neither of these cases were a permanent state of dwelling, but were the Holy Spirit choosing to abide in specific locations for specific times. Let me break here to say that I agree with many of the skeptics in not believing that many people reading these passages ignorant of the New Testament and its revelation would conclude that the Holy Spirit was a separate person or anything other than a force from God. However, when read through the lens of the Church—that is, the revelation of the incarnation and indwelling of the Holy Spirit within us—we can see how the Holy Spirit was already at work in the Old Covenant. However, this temporary indwelling of those in the Tanakh is in complete contrast to the New Testament where the bodies of believers have become the permanent abiding place of the Holy Spirit:

> Or do you not know that your body is a temple of the Holy Spirit within you, whom you have from God? You are not your own, for you were bought with a price. So glorify God in your body.
> —1 Corinthians 6:19-20 ESV

> Now Moses was faithful in all God's house as a servant, to testify to the things that were to be spoken later, but Christ is faithful over God's house as a son. And we are his house, if indeed we hold fast our confidence and our boasting in our hope.
> —Hebrews 3:5-6 ESV

Through the unfolding of the Book of Acts, we see the promise of Jesus made in Acts 1:8 that the Apostles were to be his witnesses in Jerusalem (Acts 2), Samaria (Acts 18), and the ends of the Earth (Acts 10-11, 19), and this is facilitated by the permanent indwelling of the Holy Spirit, known as *baptism of the Holy Spirit* (Matt 3:11). And through this permanent indwelling within Christians, the Holy Spirit operates his ministry in particular ways that necessitate him being a sentient, personal being. The following are some of the ways in which the Holy Spirit operates:

- John 3:5—The Holy Spirit regenerates people.
- John 14:26—The Holy Spirit teaches.
- 1 Cor 2:13—The Holy Spirit teaches.
- Acts 8:29—The Holy Spirit speaks.
- Acts 13:2—The Holy Spirit makes decisions.
- Acts 15:28—The Holy Spirit has individuality/opinions.
- John 16:13—The Holy Spirit guides.

- Eph 4:30—The Holy Spirit has feelings.
- Hebrews 10:29—The Holy Spirit can be offended/outraged.
- Acts 5:3-4—The Holy Spirit can be lied to personally.
- Acts 16:6-7—The Holy Spirit can forbid speech and actions.
- 1 Cor 12:11—The Holy Spirit distributes spiritual gifts.
- Romans 8:26-27—The Holy Spirit intercedes for us.
- 2 Timothy 3:16—The Holy Spirit inspired scripture.
- John 16:14—The Holy Spirit glorifies Jesus.
- Romans 15:30—The Holy Spirit loves.

It would seem then that Jeremiah's prophecy has proven true in saying that God has now chosen to dwell within us as the person of the Holy Spirit, not to complete some task and then take leave, but to set up permanent residency while writing his laws on our hearts. Now, no Christian shall ever have to say to another Christian, "know the Lord," because we will all know him through the permanent indwelling of the Holy Spirit within us (Jer 31:34; Heb 8:11).

## Conclusion

I would like to echo my concern as expressed within the introduction of this chapter: I remain concerned for those who stand unconvinced that the Holy Spirit is not the third person of the triune God. This concerns me because I believe that only through an accurate, biblical understanding of the personal nature of the Holy Spirit can we better embrace and know him who dwells within us than if we believe him to just be a force or tool given to us from God, which we then use to accomplish the tasks set before us. By recognizing the personhood of the Holy Spirit, Christians can say confidently that the work we do as the hands and feet of Christ are accomplished not through our own efforts using some sort of tool bestowed upon us, but done by a personal God within us and through us. Through the power and guidance of our advocate the Holy Spirit, Christians are equipped to be the witnesses of Christ to Judea, Samaria, and the ends of the Earth. I believe that by recognizing the divine personhood of the Holy Spirit and our dependent and communal relationship with him, we are better equipped to share our God with the world who does not know him.

# CHAPTER 6
# CLOSING THOUGHTS

As I close out this book, I look back through my time as an evangelical Christian and can clearly see moments where things about my faith finally "clicked" for me. The moment I finally realized that this "Trinity" thing my pastors spoke of was more than just something Christians accepted and repeated was the moment I realized that God is more complex than I had ever imagined him being. Growing up, I wrestled with the idea of God and Jesus, but looking back I was clearly distinguishing between them as two different gods rather than two persons of one God; I didn't even consider the fact that the Holy Spirit (known to me as the Holy Ghost at the time) was himself also a person of the Godhead. But after leaving for college and enrolling in my first academic Bible class, my eyes were opened to the reality that God exists not as I do, as one being (human) and one person (Joshua), but as one being (God) and three persons (Father, Son, & Spirit). My desire to know God more began the day I realized I had completely misunderstood him my entire life.

Now, I am a Bible teacher, a seminary student, and man who still after 13 years seeks to know not only about God, but to know God personally, and I believe that one who continues to grow in his or her knowledge *about* God and who he is will continue to grow in personal relationship with him. It is my hope that this book has and will continue to help you grow in your knowledge about God so that you can then grow deeper in your relationship with him. Do I believe that one must be a trinitarian in order to be saved? Absolutely not. But what I do believe is that after God has saved us, it is imperative that we continue

## Closing Thoughts

to grow in knowledge and discernment so that we may approve what is excellent, including the nature of our God as revealed to us in his word.

> And it is my prayer that your love may abound more and more, with knowledge and all discernment, so that you may approve what is excellent, and so be pure and blameless for the day of Christ, filled with the fruit of righteousness that comes through Jesus Christ, to the glory and praise of God.
> —Philippians 1:9-11 ESV

My prayer for you is the same as the Apostle Paul's was for the Philippians. May you continue to grow in your faith and understanding. God bless you.

www.ingramcontent.com/pod-product-compliance
Lightning Source LLC
Chambersburg PA
CBHW060355050426
42449CB00011B/2993